MONEY MANAGEMENT

The Path to Prosperity: Simple Strategies for Budgeting, Saving, and Growing Wealth

Larry Bishop

Copyright ©2024 by Larry Bishop

All rights reserved.

No part of this publication may be reproduced, distributed, or transmitted in any form or by any means, including photocopying, recording, or other electronic or mechanical methods, without the prior written permission of the publisher, except in the case of brief quotations embodied in critical reviews and certain other noncommercial uses permitted by copyright law.

Table of Content

INTRODUCTION 7
    Welcome To Your Financial Journey 7
    The Emotional Roller Coaster of Financial Management 7
    Why This Book is Your Companion for Financial Freedom 8

CHAPTER 1: UNDERSTANDING MONEY MANAGEMENT 11
    Definition of Money Management 11
    Money Psychology: How Emotions Influence Financial Decisions 12
    Historical Perspective: Money Management Throughout the Ages 14
    The Essentials of Money Management: A Personal Reflection 16

CHAPTER 2: POTENTIALS OF MONEY MANAGEMENT 19
    Unlocking your Financial Potential 19
    The Power of Compound Interest: Converting Time into Wealth 20
    What Does Financial Independence Really Mean? 21
    Unlocking Your Financial Potential: A Personal Commitment 22
    Role of Education and Continuous Learning 23
    Inspiring Stories: Making Potential a Reality 24
    Conclusion: Realize Your Financial Potential 26

CHAPTER 3: THE BENEFITS OF EFFECTIVE MONEY MANAGEMENT 27
    Peace of Mind: Financial and Emotional Wellbeing ... 27
    Building a Legacy: Creating Wealth for Future Generations 28

The Joy of Giving: How Financial Stability Encourages Generosity 30

Emotional Fulfillment: Achieving Personal Goals 31

Creating Opportunities: Financial Freedom and Flexibility 33

The Ripple Effect: A Positive Impact on Others 34

Conclusion: The Overall Benefits of Effective Money Management 35

CHAPTER 4: THE FOUNDATION OF BUDGETING.. 37

Crafting a Personal Budget: Your Blueprint for Financial Success 37

Emotional Spending: Recognizing and Overcoming It.. 39

Tools and Techniques: Modern Budgeting Methods.. 41

The Psychological Benefits of Budgeting 43

Inspiring Stories: The Transformative Power of Budgeting 45

Conclusion: Embracing the Power of Budgeting 47

CHAPTER 5: THE ART OF SAVING: CREATING A FINANCIAL SAFETY NETWORK 49

The Value of Saving: A Lifeline for Your Financial Well-being 49

Setting up an Emergency Fund: Your First Line of Defense 50

Short-Term Savings: Preparing for Immediate Goals. 51

Long-term Savings: Creating Wealth for the Future... 52

The Psychology of Saving: Overcoming Barriers 54

Inspiring Stories: The Transformational Power of Saving 55

Conclusion: Embrace the Art of Saving 57

CHAPTER 6: THE POWER OF INVESTING: GROWING YOUR WEALTH 59

The Essence of Investing: Making Your Money Work
for You... 59
Understanding Investment Options: Navigating the
Financial Landscape...60
The Risk-Return Tradeoff: Balancing Safety and
Growth... 63
The Emotional Side of Investing: Staying the Course 65
Inspiring Stories: The Transformative Impact of
Investing...67
Conclusion: Embracing the Power of Investing......... 69

**CHAPTER 7: ACHIEVING FINANCIAL
INDEPENDENCE.. 71**

The Journey to Financial Independence: Steps and
Milestones.. 71
Real-life Stories: Inspiring Journeys of Financial
Freedom... 75
Maintaining Financial Independence: Continuing the
Path...77

**CHAPTER 8: ADVANCED MONEY MANAGEMENT
STRATEGIES.. 81**

Tax Planning: Maximizing Your Returns....................81
Estate Planning: Securing Your Legacy.......................84
Retirement Planning: Ensuring a Comfortable Future 87

**CHAPTER 9: NAVIGATING FINANCIAL
CHALLENGES..93**

Coping with Financial Setbacks: Building Resilience 93
Debt Management: Strategies for Paying Down Debt 96
Rebuilding After Financial Hardship.......................... 99
An Inspiring Story: Rising from Financial Ruin....... 102
Conclusion... 103

**CHAPTER 10: EMOTIONAL AND
PSYCHOLOGICAL ASPECTS OF MONEY
MANAGEMENT.. 105**

    The Money-Mind Connection: Understanding Your Financial Behaviors..105

    Financial Therapy: Seeking Help When Needed...... 108

    Cultivating a Positive Money Mindset..................... 110

    An Inspiring Story: Transforming Financial Mindsets... 113

    Conclusion..115

CHAPTER 11: MONEY MANAGEMENT IN RELATIONSHIPS.. 117

    Communicating About Money: Building Trust and Understanding... 117

    Joint Finances: Strategies for Couples and Families 120

    Teaching Children About Money: Raising Financially Savvy Kids.. 122

    Inspiring Story: A Family's Financial Journey......... 125

    Conclusion... 127

CONCLUSION.. 129

    Reflecting on Your Financial Journey......................129

    Embracing a Future of Financial Freedom............... 130

    Your Ongoing Relationship with Money.................. 131

    An Inspiring Story: Jessica's Journey to Financial Empowerment.. 132

    Final Thoughts.. 133

INTRODUCTION

Welcome To Your Financial Journey

Starting on the path of money management is like setting sail on a large, undiscovered ocean. Each wave symbolizes an opportunity, each storm a challenge, and each quiet day an opportunity to contemplate and steer toward your financial objectives. This book serves as a compass, guiding you through the complexities of budgeting, investing, and achieving financial freedom. Together, we shall manage the turbulent tides and arrive at the shores of financial stability and independence.

The Emotional Roller Coaster of Financial Management

Money is more than simply numbers in a bank account or cash in your wallet; it is inextricably linked with our emotions, dreams, and anxieties. The satisfaction of a well-earned paycheck, the stress of unforeseen bills, the pride of a rising investment portfolio, and the anxiety of debt all influence our financial decisions and lives. Understanding and regulating these emotions is an important part of handling your finances.

In this book, we'll look at the psychological sides of money, assisting you in recognizing and harnessing the emotional forces at play. Whether it's the joy of reaching a financial milestone or the relief of paying off a large debt, we'll look at how to use these emotional experiences as effective motivators for your financial success.

Why This Book is Your Companion for Financial Freedom

You are not alone on this path. Millions of individuals worldwide confront comparable financial struggles and objectives. This book was developed with you in mind—a fellow traveler looking to improve your relationship with money and secure a better future. It is a partner who comprehends the nuances of human emotions and the complexity of financial systems.

We take a holistic approach, combining practical advice with emotional support. We will provide you with actionable methods to take charge of your finances, such as developing a budget and making wise investments. Along the process, we'll share tales about people who've altered their financial lives, providing inspiration and lessons learned.

As you turn these pages, remember that you are going on a revolutionary adventure. Money management is more than just amassing wealth; it's also about finding peace of mind, leaving a legacy, and empowering yourself to live the life you want. This book is your guide, mentor, and friend, and it is here to help you every step of the journey.

Let us begin this trip together. Your financial future is full of opportunities and promise. Accept it with confidence and resolve, and let the journey of money management take you to a life of freedom and fulfillment.

CHAPTER 1: UNDERSTANDING MONEY MANAGEMENT

Definition of Money Management

Money management is more than just controlling your funds; it is the art of making sound financial decisions. It includes budgeting, saving, investing, and long-term financial planning. At its foundation, money management is the act of determining where your money comes from, where it goes, and how it may best serve you. This skill establishes a foundation for financial security and progress, allowing you to confidently pursue your aspirations and negotiate life's uncertainties.

Imagine standing at the helm of your financial ship, charts in hand, plotting a course toward a destination of financial security. Money management is your map and compass, guiding you through the often turbulent waters of income, expenses, debt, and investments. It's about making intentional choices that align with your goals, values, and dreams.

Money Psychology: How Emotions Influence Financial Decisions

Money is extremely personal and emotional. Our financial decisions are frequently influenced by our emotions, beliefs, and previous experiences. Understanding the psychology of money is critical for successful financial management.

Have you ever had a rush of excitement after making an impulsive purchase, only to later feel buyer's remorse? Or the fear of checking your bank account after a costly month?

These emotions are strong and can have a substantial impact on your financial decisions.

Recognizing these emotional triggers is the first step toward making more informed financial decisions.

Let's explore some frequent emotional influences:

- ❖ **Fear and Anxiety:** The fear of not having enough money can cause stress and rash financial actions. Anxiety about future expenses might lead to oversaving and underspending, robbing you of current pleasures.
- ❖ **Joy and Rewards:** Positive feelings associated with spending might lead to overindulgence. The thrill of receiving a reward can justify unwarranted expenses, affecting your long-term financial health.
- ❖ **Guilt and Regret:** Feeling bad about prior financial blunders can impair your decision-making. It is critical to learn

from these experiences and continue forward with a positive attitude.

Understanding these emotional dynamics allows you to create more successful money management strategies that balance emotional satisfaction and financial prudence.

Historical Perspective: Money Management Throughout the Ages

Money management has changed dramatically over the years, influenced by cultural, economic, and technical developments. Understanding this history can provide important insights into our current financial habits and the reasons for them.

In ancient times, trading was the principal method of exchange. People exchanged goods and services based on their common needs and perceived value. As cultures became more complicated, coins and currency were established to facilitate trade and the accumulation of wealth. Banking systems emerged throughout the Renaissance, revolutionizing money management by providing for safer wealth storage and the introduction of credit.

The Industrial Revolution resulted in substantial economic changes, including the birth of personal finance as we know it today. People required new ways to manage their money as their access to jobs and earnings rose, resulting in the development of savings accounts, investments, and insurance.

In the present day, technology has altered money management once more. Digital banking, internet investments, and financial apps have made handling money easier and more simple than ever before. However, this convenience introduces additional concerns, such as cybersecurity risks and the requirement for digital knowledge.

Reflecting on this historical voyage, we may recognize the developments in money management and the ongoing need to adjust to changing conditions. Just as our forefathers negotiated their financial landscapes, we must too traverse the complexity of our current financial world with knowledge and judgment.

The Essentials of Money Management: A Personal Reflection

At its core, financial management is about empowerment. It's about taking charge of your financial future, making educated choices, and aligning your financial activities with your own beliefs and aspirations. It's more than simply numbers; it's about the life you want to build for yourself and your loved ones.

Consider the peace of mind that comes with knowing you have a good financial plan, the delight of seeing your savings increase, and the pride in making investments that will safeguard your future. Consider having the freedom to make decisions that correspond with your passions and the ability to weather financial storms with confidence. This is the promise of smart financial management.

As we embark on this adventure together, keep in mind that you are designing your own destiny, not just managing your money. Accept this opportunity with open arms and a determined heart. The path to financial mastery is within grasp, and this book will help you every step of the way.

CHAPTER 2: POTENTIALS OF MONEY MANAGEMENT

Unlocking your Financial Potential

Consider standing on the verge of a massive, untapped wellspring of possibility. This is what efficient money management provides. By leveraging the power of excellent financial practices, you can open up new options that were previously out of reach. It's about more than just acquiring wealth; it's about creating possibilities, safeguarding your future, and realizing your goals.

Financial potential refers to the ability to make your money work for you, allowing it to expand and increase over time. It's about taking proactive steps now to ensure a prosperous future. Consider your funds to be a seed that, with the right care and attention, may blossom into a thriving tree that provides shade, fruit, and shelter. Understanding and embracing the possibilities of your financial resources can alter your life and the lives of people around you.

The Power of Compound Interest: Converting Time into Wealth

Albert Einstein once described compound interest as the "eighth wonder of the world." The notion is simple, but the impact is deep. Compound interest is the process by which your money generates interest, which then earns more interest, resulting in a snowball effect that can considerably increase your wealth over time.

Consider this: If you invest $1,000 at a 5% annual interest rate, you will have $1,050 after one year. The following year, you get interest not just on the original $1,000, but also on the $50 interest earned the previous year, and so on.

Over time, this compounding effect grows, transforming little, persistent investments into significant wealth.

The earlier you begin investing, the greater the impact of compound interest. Time is an important factor. Even small payments can accumulate into large sums if given enough time to compound. This emphasizes the necessity of starting your financial journey early and staying focused on your long-term goals.

What Does Financial Independence Really Mean?

Many people strive for financial independence, which allows them to live their lives on their own terms without being tied to a paycheck. It's the moment at which your assets and passive income streams meet your living expenditures, freeing you up to pursue your interests, travel, spend time with loved ones, or even retire early.

To achieve financial independence, you must be disciplined, strategic, and have a clear picture of your future. It entails putting long-term benefits over short-term pleasures and making informed decisions that are consistent with your financial objectives. The trip may be difficult, but the benefits are plentiful.

Imagine waking up every day with the flexibility to decide how you spend your time. Consider the relief of knowing your finances are secure, regardless of economic volatility or unforeseen life occurrences. This is the essence of financial independence: a life full of options, possibilities, and peace of mind.

Unlocking Your Financial Potential: A Personal Commitment

The path to reaching your financial potential begins with a deliberate decision to take charge of your finances. It is about acknowledging that you have the ability to affect your financial future and making the deliberate decision to act. This commitment entails establishing specific financial goals, educating oneself on money management, and continuously following smart financial ideas.

Set your sights on both short- and long-term objectives. Paying off debt, creating an emergency fund, or saving for a large purchase are all examples of short-term goals. Long-term goals may include saving for retirement, acquiring a property, or reaching financial independence. Breaking down your goals into manageable steps allows you to make consistent progress while remaining motivated.

Role of Education and Continuous Learning

In the ever-changing world of finance, continuous learning is essential. Keep up with the latest financial trends, investment opportunities, and economic changes. Seek out books, articles, podcasts, and courses that will broaden your financial knowledge and skills. The more you understand, the more prepared you will be to make informed decisions that increase your financial potential.

Education is more than just learning knowledge; it is about empowering oneself to act. Each new understanding gives you the confidence to face financial obstacles and embrace opportunities. Adopt a lifelong learning mindset and allow it to propel you toward your financial goals.

Inspiring Stories: Making Potential a Reality

Throughout history, countless people have used their financial resources to build amazing lives. Their stories serve as powerful reminders of what is possible when you commit to sound financial management.

Consider the story of Warren Buffett, one of the world's most successful investors. Buffett began investing at an early age, using the power of compound interest and making intelligent, disciplined investment selections. His journey from humble beginnings to billionaire status exemplifies the transformative power of good financial practices.

Another inspiring example is Oprah Winfrey, who overcame significant challenges to establish a media empire. Through careful financial decisions, hard effort, and a devotion to her goal, Winfrey converted her financial potential into a reality, gaining financial independence and creating a lasting legacy.

These stories remind us that financial success is within reach for anyone willing to embrace the principles of money management and commit to their financial journey

Conclusion: Realize Your Financial Potential

As we close this chapter, take time to consider the enormous potential that exists inside your financial resources. Understanding the power of compound interest, aiming for financial independence, and committing to continuous learning will help you realize this potential and improve your financial destiny.

Take on this road with determination and optimism. Every step you take toward good money management puts you closer to reaching your financial goals. Remember that you can direct your financial destiny and live a life of plenty, freedom, and fulfillment. Let us continue this adventure together, discovering new opportunities and realizing your financial goals.

CHAPTER 3: THE BENEFITS OF EFFECTIVE MONEY MANAGEMENT

Peace of Mind: Financial and Emotional Wellbeing

Imagine waking up every day with a solid sense of security about your financial future. This peace of mind is one of the most significant advantages of good money management. When you have control over your finances, you can reduce the stress and anxiety of financial uncertainty. You can confidently confront unforeseen expenses and life's obstacles because you have a solid financial foundation to support you.

Financial security means more than just having enough money to cover your bills. It means having an emergency fund for unexpected events, insurance to protect against life's uncertainties, and a plan for future financial goals. This security allows you to live with less worry, focusing on what truly matters—your family, your passions, and your dreams.

Consider the emotional relief of knowing you're prepared for life's inevitable surprises. Whether it's a sudden medical expense, a job loss, or a major home repair, having a financial cushion can make these situations less daunting. Effective money management provides you with the tools and strategies to build this cushion, ensuring you're ready for whatever comes your way.

Building a Legacy: Creating Wealth for Future Generations

Effective money management isn't just about benefiting your life; it's also about creating a lasting legacy for your loved ones. By managing your finances wisely, you can build wealth that can be passed down to future generations, providing them with opportunities and security. This legacy is more than just money; it's the values and principles you instill in your children and grandchildren about financial responsibility and stewardship.

Imagine the pride of knowing that your financial decisions today will positively impact your family for years to come. Whether it's funding your children's education, helping them buy their first home, or ensuring they have a financial safety net, your efforts to manage money effectively will leave a lasting mark on their lives.

Building a legacy also means educating your family about money management. Share your knowledge and experiences with them, teaching them the importance of budgeting, saving, investing, and planning for the future. By doing so, you empower them to continue the legacy of financial responsibility and success.

The Joy of Giving: How Financial Stability Encourages Generosity

One of the most satisfying components of successful money management is the capacity to donate generously. When your finances are in order, you are free to support the causes and communities that are most important to you. This generosity not only benefits others, but it also provides you great joy and fulfillment in your own life.

Consider the joy that comes from making a difference in someone else's life. Whether you're donating to a charity, supporting a local business, or assisting a friend in need, your financial stability allows you to contribute with a generous heart. This act of generosity has a multiplier effect, spreading positivity and hope far beyond the initial gift.

Financial stability also allows you to volunteer your time and skills, further enriching your community. When you're not preoccupied with financial worries, you can dedicate more energy to the causes you care about. This combination of financial and personal contributions makes a powerful impact, enhancing your sense of purpose and connection to the world around you.

Emotional Fulfillment: Achieving Personal Goals

Effective money management empowers you to achieve your personal goals, leading to a deep sense of emotional fulfillment. Whether it's traveling the world, starting a business, pursuing a hobby, or buying your dream home, having control over your finances makes these dreams attainable.

Imagine the exhilaration of ticking off items from your bucket list, knowing that your financial planning and discipline have made it possible. This sense of accomplishment boosts your self-esteem and motivates you to set and achieve even more ambitious goals. Each milestone reached is a testament to your hard work and determination, fueling a cycle of positivity and progress in your life.

Personal goals aren't just about big, life-changing events; they also include everyday joys and comforts. Effective money management allows you to enjoy life's simple pleasures, from dining out with friends to enjoying a spontaneous weekend getaway. These experiences enrich your life, adding joy and satisfaction to your daily routine.

Creating Opportunities: Financial Freedom and Flexibility

One of the greatest benefits of effective money management is the financial freedom and flexibility it provides. When you manage your money well, you open up a world of opportunities that might otherwise be out of reach. This freedom allows you to make choices that align with your values and aspirations, rather than being constrained by financial limitations.

Imagine having the flexibility to pursue a career change, start your own business, or take a sabbatical to focus on personal growth. Effective money management provides the financial stability and resources to explore these opportunities without jeopardizing your security. This freedom empowers you to live life on your terms, making decisions that reflect your true passions and goals.

Financial flexibility also means being able to adapt to changing circumstances. Life is unpredictable, and having a solid financial plan allows you to navigate these changes with ease. Whether it's relocating for a new job, supporting a family member in need, or taking advantage of an unexpected opportunity, your financial stability gives you the freedom to make decisions that best serve your long-term well-being.

The Ripple Effect: A Positive Impact on Others

Your dedication to efficient money management benefits more than just you; it has a beneficial impact on everyone around you. When you are financially secure, you may offer advice and encouragement to friends and family, assisting them in achieving their own financial goals.

Your example is a significant source of inspiration, demonstrating what is achievable with dedication and practice.

Consider the impact you have in your community. By supporting local businesses, volunteering, and donating to causes you care about, you can help your town thrive and prosper. Your financial stability allows you to be a force for good, having a positive impact well beyond your personal life.

Conclusion: The Overall Benefits of Effective Money Management

As we complete this chapter, take time to consider the overall benefits of smart money management. It's about more than just acquiring wealth; it's about finding peace of mind, leaving a legacy, encouraging charity, reaching personal goals, creating possibilities, and positively impacting others. Each of these perks improves your life by adding depth, significance, and satisfaction to your financial journey.

Accept these rewards with an open heart and a determined spirit. Effective money management is a valuable instrument that can significantly improve your life. By committing to good financial habits, you can reap these rewards and create a future full of richness, independence, and fulfillment. Let us continue this adventure together, uncovering new opportunities and realizing your financial goals.

CHAPTER 4: THE FOUNDATION OF BUDGETING

Crafting a Personal Budget: Your Blueprint for Financial Success

Imagine you're about to build your dream house. You wouldn't just start laying bricks randomly—you'd follow a detailed blueprint, right? Budgeting is the blueprint for your financial life. It's the foundation upon which you build your financial future, providing a clear plan for how to allocate your resources to achieve your goals.

Creating a personal budget involves tracking your income and expenses, setting financial goals, and making a plan to reach those goals. It's about making intentional decisions with your money, ensuring that every dollar has a purpose. A well-crafted budget helps you live within your means, save for the future, and avoid the stress of financial uncertainty.

To start, list all your sources of income. This might include your salary, side gigs, investments, and any other streams of revenue. Next, categorize and track your expenses. Be thorough—include everything from rent and utilities to groceries and entertainment. This process might seem tedious, but it's essential for understanding where your money is going and identifying areas where you can cut back.

After taking a close look at your income and expenses, it's crucial to set financial objectives that are not only realistic but deeply meaningful to you. These goals should be clear and specific, something you can measure, achievable within your means, relevant to your life's priorities, and bound by a timeline to keep you focused and motivated—what we call SMART goals. Your budget isn't just a list of numbers; it's your personalized road map to a more secure and fulfilling future. It's a tool that empowers you to take control of your financial destiny, step by step, as you work towards goals that truly matter to you.

Emotional Spending: Recognizing and Overcoming It

We've all been there—splurging on an expensive dinner after a tough week, buying clothes we don't need because they were on sale, or treating ourselves to the latest gadget as a reward. Emotional spending is a common pitfall that can derail even the best budgeting plans. It's driven by our emotions rather than our needs, and it often leads to regret and financial stress.

Recognizing the triggers that lead to emotional spending is the first step in overcoming it. These triggers can vary from person to person but often include stress, boredom, sadness, or even happiness. Pay attention to your spending habits and notice if certain emotions consistently lead to impulsive purchases.

Once you've identified your triggers, develop strategies to manage them. This might involve finding alternative ways to cope with emotions, such as exercising, journaling, or talking to a friend. Establishing a waiting period before making a purchase can also help curb impulsive spending. If you still want the item after a few days or weeks, you can consider it a more deliberate and thoughtful decision.

Creating a budget that includes a small allowance for discretionary spending can also help. This allows you to enjoy occasional treats without feeling guilty or derailing your financial goals. The key is to strike a balance between responsible budgeting and allowing yourself the freedom to enjoy life's pleasures.

Tools and Techniques: Modern Budgeting Methods

In today's digital age, there are countless tools and techniques available to help you manage your budget more effectively. From apps to spreadsheets, these resources can simplify the budgeting process and provide valuable insights into your financial habits.

Budgeting tools such as Mint, YNAB (You Need a Budget), and PocketGuard help automate the process of recording income and expenses, classifying transactions, and measuring your progress toward financial objectives. These apps frequently include features such as bill reminders, expenditure alerts, and tailored financial advice, making it easier to stay on target.

If you prefer a more hands-on approach, creating a budget spreadsheet can be an effective method. Programs like Microsoft

Excel or Google Sheets offer templates that you can customize to fit your specific needs. Spreadsheets allow you to have complete control over your budget and make adjustments as needed.

Envelope budgeting is another popular technique, especially for those who prefer a cash-based system. With this method, you allocate a certain amount of cash to different spending categories (e.g., groceries, entertainment, gas) and place the money in labeled envelopes. Once an envelope is empty, you can't spend any more in that category until the next budgeting period. This method can help you become more disciplined with your spending and better understand your financial limits.

Regardless of the tools and techniques you choose, the most important aspect of budgeting is consistency. Regularly reviewing and adjusting your budget ensures that it remains aligned with your financial goals and adapts to changes in your income or expenses.

The Psychological Benefits of Budgeting

Budgeting is not just about managing money; it's also about managing your mindset. The psychological benefits of budgeting are significant and can greatly improve your overall well-being.

Creating and sticking to a budget fosters a sense of control and empowerment. It shifts your mindset from reactive to proactive, allowing you to make deliberate choices with your money rather than being driven by impulse or circumstance. This sense of control can reduce financial stress and anxiety, leading to a more positive outlook on life.

Budgeting encourages self-discipline and delayed reward. It teaches you to prioritize long-term goals over short-term pleasures, so increasing your financial resilience and patience. Over time, these talents can have a favorable impact on other aspects of your life, including your health, relationships, and personal development.

Meeting your financial goals gives you a sense of accomplishment, which is another important psychological advantage. Each milestone you hit, whether it's saving a specific amount, paying off a debt, or sticking to your spending limitations, strengthens your ability to handle your finances efficiently. This raises your confidence and encourages you to continue working toward your financial goals.

Inspiring Stories: The Transformative Power of Budgeting

Real-life stories of individuals who have transformed their financial lives through budgeting can serve as powerful sources of inspiration and motivation. These stories illustrate the tangible benefits of effective budgeting and demonstrate that financial success is achievable for anyone willing to put in the effort.

Consider the case of Ruth, a single mother who was struggling to make ends meet. With mounting debt and no savings, she felt overwhelmed and hopeless. Determined to change her situation, Ruth created a strict budget and tracked every expense. She made sacrifices, cutting out unnecessary spending and finding ways to increase her income. Over time, she paid off her debt, built an emergency fund, and even started saving for her children's education. Today, Ruth enjoys financial stability and the peace of mind that comes with it.

Then there's John, who was living paycheck to paycheck despite earning a decent salary. His wake-up call came when he realized he had no savings and was heavily reliant on credit cards. John decided to take control of his finances by creating a detailed budget. He used a budgeting app to track his spending, set financial goals, and monitor his progress. Through consistent effort and discipline, John was able to save a significant portion of his income, invest in his future, and achieve financial independence.

These stories highlight the transformative power of budgeting. They show that no matter where you start, with determination and the right strategies, you can take control of your financial future and achieve your goals.

Conclusion: Embracing the Power of Budgeting

As we conclude this chapter, it's clear that budgeting is the cornerstone of effective money management. It provides a roadmap for achieving your financial goals, helps you avoid emotional spending, and offers numerous psychological benefits. By leveraging modern tools and techniques, you can make the budgeting process more manageable and tailored to your needs.

Embrace the power of budgeting with an open heart and a determined spirit. Remember, every step you take towards creating and sticking to a budget brings you closer to financial stability, freedom, and fulfillment. Let's continue this journey together, building a solid financial foundation that supports your dreams and aspirations.

CHAPTER 5: THE ART OF SAVING: CREATING A FINANCIAL SAFETY NETWORK

The Value of Saving: A Lifeline for Your Financial Well-being

Consider your financial life a voyage across an unexpected landscape. There will be sunny days and beautiful skies, as well as thunderstorms and unexpected detours. In these uncertain times, a strong savings strategy serves as a safety net, providing you with the stability and peace of mind you need to go through whatever life throws at you.

Saving money entails more than just laying away cash; it is a disciplined habit that prepares you for your future. It's about having a buffer for crises, opportunities, and long-term objectives. A well-established savings habit allows you to cover unexpected expenses without jeopardizing your financial stability. It is the foundation of financial stability and freedom.

Setting up an Emergency Fund: Your First Line of Defense

An emergency fund is a key component of any savings plan. It is a predetermined sum of money set aside specifically for unanticipated circumstances such as medical emergencies, car repairs, or job loss. This fund is your first line of defense against financial setbacks, acting as a buffer to prevent you from emptying your long-term savings or incurring debt.

Setting a realistic goal is the first step in creating an emergency fund. Financial gurus frequently suggest saving three to six months' worth of living expenses. This amount provides a significant cushion while remaining affordable for the majority of consumers. If saving this much money appears onerous, start with a modest goal, such as $1,000, and gradually increase it over time.

Automate your savings to simplify the process. Set up a separate savings account and have a portion of your pay automatically sent each month. This method of "putting funds aside for yourself first" guarantees that saving becomes a regular habit, rather than an afterthought.

Short-Term Savings: Preparing for Immediate Goals

Short-term savings are funds set aside for expenses you anticipate in the near future, typically within the next one to five years. These might include vacations, holiday gifts, home renovations, or a new car. Having dedicated short-term savings helps you manage these costs without disrupting your monthly budget or tapping into long-term savings.

Start by identifying your short-term goals and estimating the costs. Break down the total amount needed into smaller, manageable monthly contributions. For example, if you plan to take a $2,400 vacation in one year, save $200 each month. Use high-yield savings accounts or money market accounts for these funds, as they offer better interest rates than regular savings accounts while keeping your money accessible.

Long-term Savings: Creating Wealth for the Future

Long-term savings are intended to meet goals that are several years or perhaps decades in the future. These may include purchasing a home, supporting your children's education, or investing for retirement. Long-term saving necessitates a systematic approach that prioritizes development and stability over time.

Begin by establishing clear and detailed long-term goals. Determine the amount of money you'll need and the time limit for completing each goal. This will allow you to calculate how much you need to save on a regular basis in order to stay on pace.

Consider using investment accounts for long-term savings. While traditional savings accounts offer safety and liquidity, they typically provide lower returns. Investments such as stocks, bonds, mutual funds, and retirement accounts like 401(k)s and IRAs offer the potential for higher returns, helping your money grow over the long term. Diversify your investments to balance risk and reward, and consult with a financial advisor if you need guidance.

The Psychology of Saving: Overcoming Barriers

Saving money consistently can be challenging, especially when there are so many temptations to spend. Understanding the psychological barriers to saving and developing strategies to overcome them is essential for building a strong savings habit.

One prevalent hurdle is the need for quick gratification above long-term advantages. It is human instinct to seek pleasure and avoid discomfort, yet this can lead to reckless spending and a lack of savings. Combat this by envisioning your long-term objectives and the benefits of financial stability. Create vision boards or write down your goals to keep them top of mind.

Another barrier is the idea that saving necessitates a high income. While a larger income can make saving easier, anyone can create a savings habit with dedication and preparation. Begin slowly and progressively raise your savings as your financial condition improves. Compound interest allows even little donations to accumulate up over time.

Automating your savings is a powerful strategy to overcome psychological barriers. By setting up automatic transfers, you remove the need for constant decision-making and reduce the temptation to spend. Treat your savings like a non-negotiable expense, just like rent or utilities.

Inspiring Stories: The Transformational Power of Saving

Hearing real-life accounts of people who have changed their lives by saving can be inspiring and motivating. These examples demonstrate the enormous impact that disciplined saving can have on meeting financial objectives and providing a sense of security.

Consider the case of Jerry and Mia, a couple who resolved to take charge of their money after discovering they had no savings and a lot of debt. They established a rigorous budget, eliminated superfluous expenses, and set up automatic payments to their savings account. Over the course of five years, they saved enough money to buy a house, pay off their debt, and establish a substantial emergency fund. They now enjoy financial stability and peace of mind, knowing they are ready for anything life throws at them.

Then there's Martha, who began saving little amounts from her part-time work while still in college. She diligently saved a portion of her earnings, even if it meant foregoing social events or luxury products. Her savings accumulated over time, and by the time she graduated, she had enough money to travel, start her own business, and even purchase a small home. Martha's experience demonstrates the importance of persistent savings and the long-term benefits it may provide.

Conclusion: Embrace the Art of Saving

As we wrap up this chapter, consider the crucial role that saving plays in obtaining financial stability and freedom. It's about creating an emergency fund, planning for short-term goals, and investing in your future.

Understanding the value of saving and devising techniques to overcome psychological barriers can help you develop a strong savings habit that benefits your financial well-being.

Embrace saving with dedication and optimism. Remember that every dollar saved represents a step toward a more secure and fulfilling future.

Let us continue this path together, creating a financial safety net that allows you to live life on your terms and pursue your aspirations.

CHAPTER 6: THE POWER OF INVESTING: GROWING YOUR WEALTH

The Essence of Investing: Making Your Money Work for You

Imagine planting a tree that, with time and care, grows into a lush, fruit-bearing marvel. Investing is much like this process. It's about planting seeds of wealth today to enjoy the fruits of financial prosperity tomorrow. When you invest, you're not just saving money; you're making your money work for you, growing it into something far greater.

Investing involves committing your money to various financial vehicles—such as stocks, bonds, mutual funds, and real estate—with the expectation of earning a return over time. Unlike saving, which often focuses on preserving capital, investing aims to generate income and capital appreciation, helping you build wealth and achieve your long-term financial goals.

The power of investing lies in its potential for compound growth. Compounding is the process where the earnings on your investments generate their own earnings, creating a snowball effect that can significantly increase your wealth over time. The earlier you start investing, the more time your money has to grow, making it crucial to begin as soon as possible, even if you start with small amounts.

Understanding Investment Options: Navigating the Financial Landscape

The world of investing offers a diverse array of options, each with its own risk and return characteristics. Understanding these options is key to building a balanced and effective investment portfolio.

Stocks: Investing in stocks means buying shares of ownership in a company. Stocks have the potential for high returns, as the value of the company can increase over time. However, they also come with higher risk, as stock prices can be volatile and fluctuate based on market conditions, company performance, and economic factors.

Bonds; are debt instruments issued by governments, municipalities, and enterprises to raise funds. When you purchase a bond, you are essentially lending money to the issuer in exchange for regular interest payments and the repayment of the bond's face value upon maturity. Bonds are often regarded as less risky than stocks, but they also provide lesser returns.

Mutual funds; combine money from various individuals to invest in a diverse portfolio of stocks, bonds, and other securities. They offer quick diversification and competent management, making them a popular choice among individual investors. Mutual funds can be actively managed, meaning a fund manager makes investing decisions, or passively managed, which means they monitor a market index.

Exchange-Traded Funds (ETFs): Similar to mutual funds, ETFs are collections of securities that track an index, sector, or asset class. ETFs are traded on stock exchanges like individual stocks and offer diversification, flexibility, and lower fees compared to mutual funds.

Real Estate Investing; is purchasing property with the goal of generating rental income or capital appreciation. Real estate can provide consistent cash flow and tax benefits, but it also necessitates significant investment, care, and upkeep.

Retirement Accounts: Tax-advantaged retirement accounts, such as 401(k)s and IRAs, are designed to help you save and invest for retirement. These accounts offer tax benefits, such as tax-deferred growth or tax-free withdrawals, making them essential components of a long-term investment strategy.

The Risk-Return Tradeoff: Balancing Safety and Growth

Investing always involves a tradeoff between risk and return. Higher potential returns come with higher risk, while lower-risk investments typically offer lower returns. Understanding and managing this tradeoff is crucial to building a successful investment portfolio.

Your risk tolerance—your ability and willingness to endure market fluctuations—plays a key role in determining your investment strategy. Factors such as your financial goals, time horizon, and personal comfort with risk should guide your investment decisions.

Diversification: One of the most effective ways to manage risk is through diversification—spreading your investments across different asset classes, sectors, and geographic regions. Diversification reduces the impact of any single investment's poor performance on your overall portfolio, helping to smooth out returns and manage risk.

Asset Allocation is the practice of separating your investing portfolio into several asset classes, such as stocks, bonds, and cash. Your risk tolerance, time horizon, and financial goals all influence the best asset mix for you.

Generally, younger investors with longer time horizons may afford to take on greater risk and invest significantly in stocks, whereas elderly investors approaching retirement may prefer a more conservative allocation with a higher share of bonds.

Regular Rebalancing: Over time, market movements can cause your asset allocation to drift from its target. Regularly rebalancing your portfolio—adjusting the proportions of different assets back to your original allocation—ensures that you maintain your desired level of risk and stay on track to achieve your financial goals.

The Emotional Side of Investing: Staying the Course

Investing can be an emotionally charged experience, especially during instances of market volatility. Fear and greed are strong emotions that can cause rash judgments and undermine your financial strategy. Staying disciplined and focused on your long-term goals is critical for effective investment.

Managing Fear: During market downturns, it's natural to feel anxious about losing money. However, reacting to short-term market fluctuations can result in selling low and missing out on subsequent recoveries. Instead, maintain a long-term perspective and remind yourself that market volatility is normal and temporary.

Avoiding Greed: On the flip side, during market booms, it's easy to get caught up in the excitement and take on excessive risk. Greed can lead to chasing hot stocks or speculative investments that may not align with your risk tolerance or long-term goals. Stick to your investment plan and avoid making decisions based solely on short-term gains.

Staying Informed: Educating yourself about investing and staying informed about market trends can help you make more confident and rational decisions. However, avoid overreacting to daily market news and focus on your long-term strategy.

Professional Guidance: If you're unsure about your investment decisions or need help managing your emotions, consider working with a financial advisor. A professional can provide objective advice, create a tailored investment plan, and help you stay disciplined during market fluctuations.

Inspiring Stories: The Transformative Impact of Investing

Hearing stories of individuals who have achieved financial success through investing can provide motivation and reassurance. These stories highlight the transformative power of investing and the rewards of disciplined, long-term strategies.

Consider the story of Cherie, who started investing in her early twenties with a modest salary. She consistently contributed to her retirement accounts, invested in a diversified portfolio of stocks and bonds, and reinvested her dividends. Over the years, her investments grew significantly, allowing her to retire early and pursue her passion for travel. Cherie's story demonstrates the power of compounding and the importance of starting early.

Then there's Michael, who began investing after a mid-life career change. Despite starting later, he diligently saved and invested a significant portion of his income in a mix of mutual funds and real estate. By maintaining a disciplined approach and focusing on long-term growth, Michael was able to build a substantial nest egg and achieve financial independence. His story shows that it's never too late to start investing and that consistent effort can yield impressive results.

Conclusion: Embracing the Power of Investing

As we conclude this chapter, reflect on the immense potential that investing holds for growing your wealth and achieving your financial goals. It's about making your money work for you, leveraging the power of compounding, and navigating the financial landscape with informed and disciplined decisions.

Embrace the power of investing with confidence and optimism. Remember, every investment decision you make is a step towards financial independence and security. Let's continue this journey together, building a robust investment portfolio that supports your dreams and aspirations, and unlocking the transformative power of growing your wealth.

CHAPTER 7: ACHIEVING FINANCIAL INDEPENDENCE

The Journey to Financial Independence: Steps and Milestones

Achieving financial independence is more than just a goal; it's a transformative journey that reshapes your relationship with money, time, and freedom. Imagine waking up each day knowing you have the freedom to pursue your passions, spend time with loved ones, and explore new opportunities without the stress of financial constraints. This chapter will guide you through the steps and milestones necessary to embark on this liberating journey.

1. **Setting Clear Financial Goals**

The first step towards financial independence is defining what it means to you. For some, it might mean retiring early, while for others, it could mean having the freedom to work on projects they love. Start by setting clear, specific, and measurable financial goals. This could include paying off debt, building an emergency fund, saving for retirement, or generating passive income.

2. Establishing a Budget and Tracking Expenses

A solid budget is the basis for financial independence. Keep thorough records of your income and expenses to better understand your spending habits. Determine where you can minimize costs and put those savings toward your financial goals. Use budgeting tools and applications to make the process easier and more efficient.

3. Eliminating Debt

Debt can be a significant obstacle to financial independence. Prioritize paying off high-interest debt, such as credit cards, as quickly as possible. Use strategies like the debt snowball or debt avalanche method to systematically reduce your debt. Once your high-interest debt is under control, focus on paying off other debts like student loans and mortgages.

4. Set up an Emergency Fund.

An emergency fund provides a financial safety net. Set aside three to six months' worth of living expenses in an easily accessible account. This fund will protect you from unexpected expenses and provide you peace of mind as you work toward financial freedom.

5. Investing Wisely

Investing is an essential part of gaining financial freedom. Create a diverse investment portfolio that is consistent with your risk tolerance and long-term objectives. Maximize contributions to retirement accounts such as 401(k)s and IRAs, as well as other investment options such as stocks, bonds, and real estate. The power of compound interest will enable your investments to expand over time.

6. Generate Passive Income

Passive income streams are critical to sustaining financial freedom. Consider options such as rental properties, dividend-paying equities, peer-to-peer lending, or developing digital products. The idea is to earn revenue that requires little effort to maintain, allowing you to focus on what is most important to you.

7. Reaching Key Milestones

Throughout your journey, celebrate key milestones. These could include paying off a significant debt, reaching a certain net worth, or achieving a specific level of passive income. Celebrating these achievements will keep you motivated and remind you of the progress you're making.

Real-life Stories: Inspiring Journeys of Financial Freedom

Real-life stories of individuals who have achieved financial independence can provide powerful inspiration and valuable insights. Here are two compelling stories of people who transformed their financial lives and achieved the freedom they desired.

1. Dora's Journey to Debt Freedom and Early Retirement

Dora, a single mother and teacher, was burdened with student loans and credit card debt. Determined to change her financial situation, she started by creating a strict budget and cutting unnecessary expenses. She took on a side hustle as a freelance writer, using the extra income to pay off her high-interest debts. Once debt-free, Dora focused on investing in her 401(k) and a Roth IRA. Over the years, her investments grew, and she reached her goal of retiring early at the age of 45. Dora now spends her time traveling, volunteering, and pursuing her passion for photography.

2. Peter and Jane's Path to Financial Independence Through Real Estate

Peter and Jane, a married couple with three children, decided to pursue financial independence through real estate investing. They started by purchasing a duplex, living in one unit while renting out the other. With the rental income covering their mortgage, they saved aggressively and reinvested their profits into additional properties. Over a decade, they built a portfolio of rental properties that generated substantial passive income. Today, Peter and Jane have achieved financial independence, allowing them to retire from their corporate jobs and spend more time with their family and community.

Maintaining Financial Independence: Continuing the Path

Achieving financial independence is a monumental accomplishment, but maintaining it requires ongoing effort and vigilance. Here are key strategies to ensure you stay on the path of financial freedom.

1. Continuous financial education.

The financial world is always evolving, with new investment opportunities, tax restrictions, and economic conditions. Endeavor to always keep up to date on investment and personal income affairs. Attend seminars, read books, stay up to date on financial news, and think about working with a financial advisor to keep your knowledge current.

2. Regular portfolio review and rebalancing

Periodically assess your investment portfolio to ensure it is in line with your objectives and risk tolerance. Rebalance your portfolio as needed to keep your desired asset allocation. To maintain your portfolio balanced, sell high-performing assets and buy low-performing ones.

3. Living Below Your Means

Even after achieving financial independence, it's crucial to live below your means. Avoid lifestyle inflation, which can erode your financial security. Continue to budget, save, and invest wisely. This disciplined approach will help you weather economic downturns and unexpected expenses.

4. Protecting Your Assets.

Protecting your assets will help you maintain financial independence. Make sure you have enough insurance coverage, which includes health, house, auto, and life insurance. Consider estate planning to safeguard your assets and care for your loved ones in the future.

5. Giving Back and Finding Purpose

Financial independence provides the freedom to pursue your passions and give back to the community. Consider how you can use your time and resources to make a positive impact. Whether through volunteering, mentoring, or philanthropy, finding purpose beyond financial success will enrich your life and provide fulfillment.

6. Staying Flexible and Adaptable

Life is unpredictable, and circumstances can change. Stay flexible and adaptable, ready to adjust your financial strategies as needed. Whether facing a market downturn, a health issue, or a major life event, maintaining a resilient mindset will help you navigate challenges while preserving your financial independence.

In conclusion, achieving and maintaining financial independence is a journey that requires dedication, education, and perseverance. By setting clear goals, managing your finances wisely, and staying adaptable, you can create a future where you have the freedom to live life on your terms. Let the inspiring stories of those who have walked this path before you serve as a reminder that financial independence is attainable, and the rewards are immeasurable.

CHAPTER 8: ADVANCED MONEY MANAGEMENT STRATEGIES

Tax Planning: Maximizing Your Returns

Tax planning is a crucial element of advanced money managemut tent. It goes beyond simply filing your tax return; it's about strategically arranging your financial affairs to minimize your tax liability while maximizing your returns. Imagine your hard-earned money being optimized to its fullest potential, where every dollar works harder for you, and your financial goals come within reach more quickly.

Understanding the Tax Brackets and Credits

Understanding tax brackets and credits is the first step toward efficient tax planning. Tax brackets are levels of income taxed at different rates, and knowing where you fall might help you prepare more effectively. Tax credits, on the other hand, immediately reduce the amount of tax owed. Familiarize yourself with common benefits such as the Earned Income Tax Credit (EITC), Child Tax Credit, and Education Credit, which can dramatically reduce your tax liability.

Maximizing Deductions and Contributions

Deductions lower your taxable income, which can result in substantial tax savings. Make sure to take advantage of deductions available to you, such as those for mortgage interest, charitable contributions, and medical expenses. Additionally, contributing to tax-advantaged accounts like 401(k)s, IRAs, and Health Savings Accounts (HSAs) can reduce your taxable income and grow your savings tax-free or tax-deferred.

Timing Income and Expenses

Strategically timing your income and expenses can have a big impact on your tax bill. For example, if you're on the verge of entering a higher tax bracket, you may postpone certain income or accelerate deductible expenses into the current year. This can reduce your taxable income for the year, keeping you in a lower bracket and lowering your total tax obligation.

Utilizing Tax-Efficient Investments

Investing in tax-efficient vehicles can further enhance your tax planning strategy. Municipal bonds, for example, offer tax-free interest income at the federal level and possibly at the state level. Additionally, holding investments in tax-advantaged accounts like Roth IRAs can help you grow your wealth without the burden of taxes on the gains.

Working with a Tax Professional

Given the complexity of the tax code, working with a tax professional can be invaluable. They can provide personalized advice, help you navigate changes in tax laws, and identify strategies that align with your financial goals. A tax professional can also assist with tax-loss harvesting, where you sell investments at a loss to offset gains, thereby reducing your taxable income.

Estate Planning: Securing Your Legacy

Estate planning is about ensuring your legacy is preserved and your loved ones are taken care of after you're gone. It involves making decisions about how your assets will be managed and distributed, and it provides peace of mind knowing that your wishes will be honored. Picture a future where your hard work and dedication continue to support your family and causes you care about, even when you're no longer here.

Developing a Will and Trust

A will is the foundation of any estate plan, stating your desires for asset distribution and the care of minor children. However, a will alone may be insufficient. Trusts can provide you more control over how and when your assets are dispersed, perhaps eliminating probate and lowering estate taxes. Revocable living trusts, for example, allow you to make modifications during your lifetime while also ensuring a smooth handover of assets.

Designating Beneficiaries

Make sure that all of your financial accounts, insurance policies, and retirement plans have current beneficiary designations. These designations often trump your will, so they must match your current preferences. Regularly evaluate and revise them, particularly after big life events such as marriage, divorce, or childbirth.

Minimizing Estate Taxes

Estate taxes can significantly reduce the amount passed on to your heirs. Strategies to minimize these taxes include gifting during your lifetime, setting up trusts, and taking advantage of the estate tax exemption limits. Gifting not only reduces the size of your estate but also allows you to see the impact of your generosity.

Planning for Incapacity

Estate planning isn't just about what happens after you die; it's also about protecting yourself and your assets if you become incapacitated. Establish a durable power of attorney to manage your finances and a healthcare proxy to make medical decisions on your behalf. Living wills and advance healthcare directives ensure your medical preferences are known and respected.

Charitable Giving

If charitable giving is important to you, incorporate it into your estate plan. Setting up a charitable trust or donor-advised fund can provide ongoing support to your favorite causes and potentially offer tax benefits. Charitable remainder trusts, for instance, allow you to receive income during your lifetime, with the remainder going to charity upon your death.

Retirement Planning: Ensuring a Comfortable Future

Retirement planning is about securing a future where you can enjoy the fruits of your labor without financial stress. Imagine a retirement where you have the freedom to travel, pursue hobbies, and spend time with loved ones. This section will guide you through the key strategies to ensure a comfortable and fulfilling retirement.

Estimating Retirement Needs

The first stage in retirement planning is determining how much you'll need to live your preferred lifestyle. Consider things like living expenses, healthcare costs, travel, and recreational activities. A general rule of thumb is to strive for 70-80% of your pre-retirement income, but individual requirements may differ. Use retirement calculators to get a more accurate picture based on your situation.

Maximizing Retirement Contributions

Take full advantage of tax-advantaged retirement accounts such as 401(k)s, IRAs, and Roth IRAs. Contribute the maximum allowed amount each year and, if your employer offers a matching contribution, ensure you're contributing enough to receive the full match. This is practically free money that can greatly increase your retirement savings.

Diversifying Retirement Investments

A diversified investment portfolio is crucial for managing risk and achieving growth. As you approach retirement, gradually shift your asset allocation towards more conservative investments to preserve your capital. However, it's important to still include growth-oriented investments to combat inflation and ensure your savings last throughout retirement.

Considering Healthcare Costs

Healthcare is one of the most expensive aspects of retirement. Plan for these costs by considering long-term care insurance and maximizing contributions to HSAs if you're eligible. Medicare will cover some of your healthcare needs, but be prepared for out-of-pocket expenses and consider supplemental insurance to fill in the gaps.

Deciding on Social Security

Deciding when to begin collecting Social Security benefits is an important part of retirement planning. While you can start receiving benefits at age 62, waiting until your full retirement age or even until age 70 can significantly increase your monthly benefit. Consider your health, financial needs, and employment status when making this decision.

Creating a Retirement Income Plan

A solid retirement income plan involves determining how you'll withdraw funds from your various accounts. The goal is to create a steady income stream that meets your needs without depleting your savings too quickly. Strategies include the 4% rule, annuities, and laddering bonds. Work with a financial advisor to develop a plan tailored to your situation.

Staying Active and Engaged

Finally, retirement planning isn't just about finances; it's also about ensuring a fulfilling lifestyle. Stay active and engaged by pursuing hobbies, volunteering, or even working part-time. A fulfilling retirement involves not just financial security, but also emotional and physical well-being.

In conclusion, advanced money management strategies are essential for maximizing your financial potential and securing a prosperous future. By mastering tax planning, estate planning, and retirement planning, you can ensure that your money works for you, your legacy is protected, and your retirement is comfortable and fulfilling. Let these strategies guide you towards a future where financial stress is minimized, and your dreams are realized.

CHAPTER 9: NAVIGATING FINANCIAL CHALLENGES

Coping with Financial Setbacks: Building Resilience

Financial setbacks can be daunting and overwhelming, shaking the very foundation of our lives. However, they also present an opportunity to build resilience and emerge stronger. Imagine a ship caught in a storm. It faces waves and winds that threaten to capsize it, but with a strong hull and skilled navigation, it can weather the storm and sail into calmer waters. This section is about equipping you with the tools and mindset to navigate financial turbulence.

1. Acknowledge and Assess the Situation

The first step in coping with a financial setback is to acknowledge the situation. Denial or avoidance can exacerbate the problem. Take a deep breath, accept the reality, and assess the extent of the setback. Whether it's a job loss, medical emergency, or investment loss, understanding the full scope will help you formulate a plan.

2. Create a New Budget

In the wake of a financial setback, it's crucial to re-evaluate your budget. Prioritize essential expenses like housing, food, utilities, and transportation. Cut non-essential spending and look for ways to reduce costs. This temporary austerity can help stabilize your finances and free up resources to address the immediate challenge.

3. Seek support and guidance.

You do not have to confront financial problems alone. Contact family, friends, or financial professionals for assistance and advice. They can provide helpful guidance, resources, and emotional support. Community organizations and government programs can also help with basic needs like food, shelter, and healthcare.

4. Develop a Recovery Plan

Once you have a clear picture of your situation and a revised budget, develop a recovery plan. Set realistic short-term and long-term goals to regain financial stability. This might include finding new employment, consolidating debt, or selling non-essential assets. Break down your ambitions into doable steps and recognize little successes along the way.

5. Cultivate a Resilient Mindset

Building financial resilience is as much about mindset as it is about money management. Cultivate a positive and proactive attitude. Learn from the setback and view it as a learning experience rather than a failure. In order to manage stress and stabilize your emotional and mental well-being, you need to take self-care exercises very important

Debt Management: Strategies for Paying Down Debt

Debt can feel like a heavy burden, but with the right strategies, you can manage and eliminate it, freeing yourself from financial stress. Imagine climbing a steep mountain; the ascent is challenging, but with each step, you get closer to the summit and the breathtaking view. Let's explore strategies to help you conquer debt.

1. Be aware of your debt.

The first step in debt management is to learn about your debt. List all of your debts, including credit cards, student loans, home loans, and personal loans. Keep track of your balances, interest rates, and minimum monthly payments. This will offer you a comprehensive picture of your total debt status.

2. Pick a Debt Repayment Strategy.

There are various successful debt repayment options. The debt snowball and debt avalanche strategies are two popular approaches:

- **Debt Snowball:** Focus on paying off the smallest debts first while making minimum payments on larger debts. Once a small debt is paid off, move to the next smallest. This method provides psychological boosts as you see debts eliminated quickly.
- **Debt Avalanche:** Prioritize paying off debts with the highest interest rates first while making minimum payments on others. This method saves more money

in interest over time and can accelerate debt repayment.

3. Negotiate with Creditors

Don't hesitate to contact your creditors and negotiate better terms. You might be able to secure lower interest rates, extended repayment periods, or even debt settlement. Creditors are often willing to work with you if it increases their chances of recovering the owed amount.

4. Consolidate Your Debt

Debt consolidation involves merging multiple loans into a single loan with a lower interest rate. By doing that, payments can be made in a step-by-step manner with a reduction in interest payable. Options for consolidation include the following; debt management plans, balance transfer credit cards, personal loans, and home equity loans/home equity lines of credit.

However, it's crucial to carefully review the terms and avoid accumulating additional debt.

5. Consider Professional Help

If you're struggling to manage your debt, consider seeking professional help from a credit counseling agency or financial advisor. They can provide tailored advice, help you create a debt management plan, and negotiate with creditors on your behalf.

Rebuilding After Financial Hardship

Rebuilding your financial life after a hardship is a journey of recovery and renewal. It's like constructing a house after a storm has passed; with a solid foundation and careful planning, you can build something stronger and more resilient. This section offers guidance on how to start anew and regain financial stability.

1. Assess and Learn from the Experience

Reflect on the financial hardship you faced. Assess what led to the situation and identify any mistakes or unforeseen events. Use this understanding to build a more robust financial plan that mitigates future risks. Learning from the past will empower you to make better decisions moving forward.

2. Re-establish Financial Goals

Set clear and achievable financial goals to guide your recovery. These goals might include rebuilding your emergency fund, paying off remaining debts, or saving for future milestones like buying a home or retiring. Break these goals into smaller, actionable steps and track your progress regularly.

3. Create an emergency fund.

One of the first steps in rebuilding is to establish or refill an emergency fund. Set aside three to six months' worth of living expenses in an easily accessible account. This fund will act as a financial cushion against future setbacks, bringing peace of mind.

4. Improve Your Financial Literacy

Enhance your financial literacy by educating yourself on personal finance topics such as budgeting, investing, and credit management. Utilize resources like books, online courses, and workshops. The more you know, the better prepared you will be to make sound financial decisions.

5. Rebuild Your Credit

If your credit took a hit during the financial hardship, focus on rebuilding it. Pay all bills on time, reduce your debt-to-income ratio, and avoid taking on new debt. Consider using a secured credit card or becoming an authorized user on someone else's account to improve your credit score gradually.

6. Invest in Your Future

As you regain financial stability, start investing in your future. Contribute to retirement accounts, diversify your investments, and consider long-term growth opportunities. Investing wisely will help you build wealth and secure your financial future.

An Inspiring Story: Rising from Financial Ruin

Megan's story is one of resilience and determination. After losing her job during an economic downturn, she faced mounting bills and debt. Feeling overwhelmed, she feared she might lose her home. However, Megan refused to give up. She sought guidance from a financial advisor who helped her create a realistic budget and debt repayment plan.

Megan cut unnecessary expenses, took on part-time work, and negotiated with her creditors. She also enrolled in financial literacy courses to better understand money management. Slowly but surely, she paid off her debts and rebuilt her savings.

Today, Megan is debt-free with a solid emergency fund and a diversified investment portfolio. She even started her own business, turning a passion into a profitable venture. Megan's journey from financial ruin to success serves as a powerful reminder that with the right strategies and a resilient mindset, it's possible to overcome financial challenges and build a brighter future.

Conclusion

Navigating financial challenges requires resilience, strategic planning, and a positive mindset. By coping effectively with setbacks, managing debt wisely, and rebuilding after hardship, you can regain control of your finances and create a stable and prosperous future. With determination and the right tools, you can weather any financial storm and come out stronger on the other side.

CHAPTER 10: EMOTIONAL AND PSYCHOLOGICAL ASPECTS OF MONEY MANAGEMENT

The Money-Mind Connection: Understanding Your Financial Behaviors

Money is not just a physical entity; it's deeply intertwined with our emotions and psychology. Our financial behaviors are often driven by underlying beliefs, habits, and experiences. Imagine a powerful river flowing through your life—sometimes calm, sometimes turbulent. Understanding the currents beneath the surface is key to navigating its course effectively.

1. Recognizing Emotional Triggers

To make good financial decisions, we need an important factor which is our emotions.

Recognizing emotional triggers, such as stress, anxiety, or excitement, can help you understand why you spend, save, or invest the way you do. For instance, some people shop to cope with stress, while others might hoard money due to fear of financial insecurity. Identifying these triggers is the first step in gaining control over your financial behaviors.

2. Exploring Financial Beliefs

Our beliefs about money are often shaped by our upbringing and cultural background. Reflect on the messages you received about money as a child. Were you taught that money is scarce and should be saved, or that it's meant to be enjoyed and spent freely? These beliefs can significantly influence your financial habits. To excel, we need to let go and fight any thoughts that hold us back and focus on thoughts that will help us excel.

3. Understanding Financial Habits

Habits are formed through repeated actions and can be hard to change. Analyze your financial habits—both good and bad. Do you consistently save a portion of your income, or do you tend to spend impulsively? Understanding these patterns will help you make conscious changes. For example, setting up automatic savings transfers can transform saving from a challenge into a habit.

4. Balancing Rational and Emotional Decisions

While it's essential to be rational in financial planning, completely ignoring emotions can lead to burnout or dissatisfaction. Find a balance between rational analysis and emotional satisfaction. Allow yourself occasional indulgences that bring joy without jeopardizing your financial goals. This balanced approach can make financial management more sustainable and fulfilling.

Financial Therapy: Seeking Help When Needed

Sometimes, managing the emotional and psychological aspects of money requires professional help. Financial therapy combines financial advice with psychological counseling to address the emotional roots of financial behaviors. Imagine having a guide to help you navigate the emotional labyrinth of money, leading you toward a healthier relationship with your finances.

1. Recognizing When You Need Help

It's important to recognize when you might need professional help. If you're experiencing chronic stress about money, frequent arguments with loved ones over finances, or patterns of self-sabotaging financial behavior, it may be time to seek assistance. A financial therapist can help you understand and address these issues.

2. What to Expect in Financial Therapy

In financial therapy, you'll explore the emotional and psychological factors influencing your financial decisions. Therapists use various techniques, such as cognitive-behavioral therapy (CBT), to help you change negative thought patterns and behaviors. You'll learn practical financial skills, like budgeting and debt management, while also addressing underlying emotional issues.

3. Finding the Right Therapist

Finding a qualified financial therapist is crucial. Look for professionals who are certified in both financial planning and therapy. Organizations like the Financial Therapy Association can help you find accredited therapists. Do your research on the techniques and results of a therapist who would attend to you, to ascertain if they align with your problems for a better result.

4. The Benefits of Financial Therapy

Financial therapy can lead to significant improvements in your financial well-being and overall quality of life. By addressing emotional barriers and developing healthier financial habits, you can reduce stress, improve relationships, and achieve your financial goals more effectively. The process can be transformative, empowering you to take control of your financial future.

Cultivating a Positive Money Mindset

A positive money mindset is essential for financial success and well-being. It involves having a healthy attitude towards money, viewing it as a tool to achieve your goals, rather than a source of stress or conflict. Imagine planting a garden where your thoughts and beliefs about money are the seeds. Cultivating a positive mindset ensures that your garden flourishes with abundance and prosperity.

1. Embracing Financial Abundance

Shift your mindset from scarcity to abundance. Believe that there are enough resources and opportunities for everyone, including yourself. This doesn't mean ignoring financial challenges but rather focusing on solutions and possibilities. Practicing gratitude for what you have can foster a sense of abundance and attract more positive financial experiences

2. Setting Empowering Financial Goals

Set clear and empowering financial goals that align with your values and aspirations. Goals provide direction and motivation. Ease yourself the pressure, identify your big goal and spread it into small pieces, and also remember to celebrate your achieved goals as you move on. This approach not only keeps you focused but also reinforces a positive mindset by showing you that financial success is achievable.

3. Practicing Mindfulness and Self-Compassion

Mindfulness involves being present and aware of your thoughts and feelings about money without judgment. It helps you make conscious financial decisions rather than reacting impulsively. Practice self-compassion by being kind to yourself when you make financial mistakes. Understand that everyone faces setbacks, and use them as learning opportunities.

4. Visualizing Financial Success

To develop a positive financial mindset, you need to employ the powerful tool of representation/imagery. Regularly visualize yourself achieving your financial goals. Imagine the feelings of security, freedom, and happiness that come with financial success. This practice can boost your motivation and align your actions with your aspirations.

An Inspiring Story: Transforming Financial Mindsets

Let's take a moment to share the story of Gabriel and Esther, a couple who transformed their financial lives by addressing the emotional and psychological aspects of money management.

Gabriel and Esther were struggling with debt and constant financial stress. Arguments about money became a regular part of their relationship. Feeling overwhelmed, they decided to seek help from a financial therapist.

Through therapy, they discovered that Gabriel's fear of scarcity stemmed from his childhood experiences of financial instability. Esther realized that her impulsive spending was a way to cope with stress and seek temporary happiness. With their therapist's guidance, they began to understand and address these underlying issues.

They learned to communicate openly about their financial concerns and set shared goals. By creating a budget and sticking to it, they started paying down their debt. They also adopted a practice of gratitude and mindfulness, which helped them focus on the positive aspects of their financial journey.

Over time, Gabriel and Esther not only improved their financial situation but also strengthened their relationship. They celebrated small victories, like paying off a credit card, and supported each other through setbacks. Their story is a testament to the power of understanding and transforming the emotional and psychological aspects of money management.

Conclusion

The emotional and psychological aspects of money management are integral to achieving financial well-being. By understanding the money-mind connection, seeking help through financial therapy when needed, and cultivating a positive money mindset, you can transform your relationship with money. Let the inspiring story of Gabriel and Esther remind you that financial challenges are not just about numbers; they are deeply personal journeys. With the right mindset and support, you can navigate these challenges, build resilience, and create a financially prosperous and emotionally fulfilling life.

CHAPTER 11: MONEY MANAGEMENT IN RELATIONSHIPS

Communicating About Money: Building Trust and Understanding

Money can be a delicate topic in relationships, often leading to conflicts and misunderstandings. However, when handled with care and open communication, it can also strengthen the bond between partners. Imagine a couple sitting down with a cup of coffee, sharing their dreams and plans. This simple act of talking about money can build trust and deepen understanding.

1. Creating a Safe Space for Discussions

The first step to effective financial communication is creating a safe, judgment-free zone. Choose a comfortable setting and a relaxed time to discuss money matters, ensuring both partners are calm and focused. Approach the conversation with empathy and patience, allowing each person to express their thoughts and feelings without interruption.

2. Practicing Transparency

Transparency is vital in financial discussions. Share your complete financial picture, including income, debts, savings, and investments. Honesty about past financial mistakes and current challenges fosters trust. Being open about your financial situation prevents hidden surprises and helps both partners understand the full scope of their finances.

3. Understanding Money Mindsets

Each person has a unique money mindset shaped by their upbringing, experiences, and personality. One partner might be someone who thinks of the future (Savings), while the other could be one who loves to lavish every and any little thing (Expenses/spends). Understanding these differences is crucial. Discuss your financial values, fears, and goals. Recognize and respect each other's perspectives, and find common ground to build a harmonious financial plan.

4. Setting Shared Financial Goals

Shared financial goals align your efforts and create a sense of partnership. Whether it's saving for a home, planning a vacation, or building an emergency fund, having mutual objectives fosters teamwork. Break down these goals into actionable steps and celebrate milestones together, reinforcing your commitment to each other.

Joint Finances: Strategies for Couples and Families

Managing joint finances requires collaboration, compromise, and clear strategies. It's like navigating a ship where both partners are co-captains, steering towards a common destination. Here are some strategies to help couples and families manage their finances effectively.

1. Choosing a Financial Management Style

Couples can choose from various financial management styles:

- **Combined Finances:** Pooling all income and expenses into joint accounts.
- **Separate Finances:** Keeping individual accounts and splitting shared expenses.
- **Hybrid Approach:** Combining both methods, with joint accounts for shared

expenses and individual accounts for personal spending.

Discuss and agree on the approach that suits your relationship best, considering your financial habits and comfort levels.

2. Creating a Joint Budget

A joint budget is essential for managing household finances. List all sources of income and categorize expenses into needs, wants, and savings. Allocate funds for each category, ensuring you meet your financial obligations while leaving room for personal spending. Regularly review and adjust the budget to accommodate changes in income or expenses.

3. Handling Debt Together

Debt can be a significant stressor in relationships. Develop a joint plan to tackle debt, prioritizing high-interest debts first. Look towards reducing your debt and collapsing them into one or try to settle with your creditors for a better arrangement. Support each other through the process, celebrating progress and staying committed to becoming debt-free together.

4. Planning for the Future

Long-term financial planning is crucial for couples and families. Discuss and plan for significant life events such as buying a home, having children, education expenses, and retirement. Set up savings accounts and investment plans to achieve these goals. Regularly revisit your plans to ensure they align with your evolving needs and aspirations.

Teaching Children About Money: Raising Financially Savvy Kids

Teaching children about money is an invaluable gift that prepares them for a secure and responsible future. Imagine a child learning to save their allowance for a toy they desire, understanding the value of patience and planning. Here are ways to raise financially savvy kids.

1. Starting Early

Introduce basic financial concepts early. Teach young children about money through play, using games and toys to simulate buying and selling. Explain the difference between needs and wants, and the importance of saving for the future. Use everyday activities, like grocery shopping, as teachable moments about budgeting and making choices.

2. Encouraging Saving and Budgeting

Encourage children to save a portion of their allowance or money they receive as gifts. Provide a piggy bank or a savings account to help them visualize their savings. Teach them to budget by dividing their money into categories like saving, spending, and sharing. This practice instills the value of saving and the discipline of budgeting.

3. Introducing Banking and Investments

Expose children to more sophisticated financial systems as they grow older. Explain how banks work, the purpose of checking and savings accounts, and the basics of interest. Consider opening a joint savings account to teach them about banking firsthand. Discuss simple investment concepts, such as stocks and bonds, and the importance of long-term financial planning.

4. Teaching Financial Responsibility

Financial responsibility includes understanding the consequences of financial decisions. Teach children about borrowing, credit, and the impact of debt. Help them to be responsible by exposing them to avenues of earning money such as through part-time jobs or doing chores, as this will also help boost their ability to be independent. Discuss the importance of charitable giving and the impact it has on the community.

Inspiring Story: A Family's Financial Journey

The Barrys family faced significant financial challenges when they lost their primary source of income. With bills piling up and stress levels high, they decided to take control of their situation together. They held family meetings to discuss their financial status openly, involving their children in the process.

Through these meetings, the children learned about budgeting, saving, and the importance of teamwork. The family created a joint budget, cutting unnecessary expenses and finding ways to increase their income. They set shared financial goals, such as paying off debt and building an emergency fund.

As the Barrys worked together, their bond strengthened. They celebrated small victories, like paying off a credit card or reaching a savings milestone. The children, seeing their parents' resilience and dedication, developed a deep understanding of financial responsibility.

Years later, the Barry family not only overcame their financial hardships but also built a secure and prosperous future.

The children, now young adults, carry the lessons they learned into their own lives, making informed financial decisions and appreciating the value of hard work and collaboration.

Conclusion

Money management in relationships is a journey of communication, collaboration, and education. By openly discussing finances, setting shared goals, and teaching children about money, you can build a strong financial foundation and foster trust and understanding in your relationships.

Remember, financial challenges can be navigated successfully with teamwork and a positive mindset. Let the inspiring story of the Johnson family remind you that, together, you can overcome any financial obstacle and create a brighter future.

CONCLUSION

Reflecting on Your Financial Journey

As you reach the end of this book, take a moment to reflect on your financial journey. Think about where you started, the challenges you've faced, and the progress you've made. Each chapter you've read and each step you've taken has brought you closer to understanding and mastering your finances.

Remember the first time you set a budget, the initial anxiety of facing your debts, or the joy of seeing your savings grow. Reflect on the conversations you've had with loved ones about money, the habits you've changed, and the goals you've achieved. Your journey has not just been about numbers; it's been about growth, resilience, and transformation.

Embracing a Future of Financial Freedom

Now, envision your future. Imagine a life where financial stress is a distant memory, where your money works for you, and your goals are within reach. Embracing financial freedom means having the confidence to make choices that align with your values and aspirations. It's about security and peace of mind, knowing you're prepared for whatever comes your way.

Picture the possibilities: traveling to places you've always dreamed of, supporting your children's education, retiring comfortably, or perhaps giving back to your community. Financial freedom allows you to live a life that's rich in experiences and opportunities. It's the culmination of all your efforts, discipline, and smart decisions.

Your Ongoing Relationship with Money

Your relationship with money is ongoing and ever-evolving. Just as in any relationship, it requires attention, care, and continuous learning. Stay curious and informed about financial matters. Revisit your goals regularly and adjust your plans as needed. Remember to celebrate the little success as you progress and take note of your mistakes and learn from them.

Remember that money is a tool, not an end in itself. It's there to support your dreams, provide for your needs, and enhance your well-being. Cultivate a positive mindset towards money, seeing it as a partner in your journey rather than a source of stress.

An Inspiring Story: Jessica's Journey to Financial Empowerment

Let's conclude with the inspiring story of Jessica, a single mother who once felt overwhelmed by her financial situation. With determination and the guidance of this book, she took charge of her finances. Jessica started by creating a budget and sticking to it. She paid off her debts, one step at a time, and began saving for her future.

Jessica's journey was not without challenges. There were moments of doubt and difficulty, but she persevered. She sought support from friends and financial advisors, educated herself on investment strategies, and gradually built a secure financial foundation. Today, Jessica not only enjoys financial freedom but also serves as a role model for her children, teaching them the value of money management.

Final Thoughts

Your journey with money management is a lifelong adventure. You have the tools, knowledge, and mindset to navigate this path successfully. Embrace the challenges and triumphs, knowing that each step you take brings you closer to financial empowerment and freedom.

As you continue your journey, remember to share your experiences and knowledge. Recommend this book to friends and family who could benefit from it. Your story, like Jessica's, can inspire others to take control of their finances and build a brighter future.

Thank you for taking this journey with us. May your financial future be one of prosperity, stability, and joy.

www.ingramcontent.com/pod-product-compliance
Lightning Source LLC
Chambersburg PA
CBHW050303230526
45471CB00005B/1996